i painted the kitchen green.

t. sloan

For the one I hope never reads it.

Table of Contents

I see you everywhere

I see you in February and March, and April and May,
and June.
But never July.

And at the gas pump on the far right and the roads that
go left and the black cars and aisle 11 and empty
parking lots
With orange letters.

And coconut pie and humming fans and the sound of a
plastic yellow box cutter hitting the floor with too
many rubber bands wrapped around it and the wall
with the flowers and the thermostat and a broken
strawberry hair brush and pretzels in the mall.
And things that are green.

And an elephant with a pink bow two days before
Valentine's Day and a dreary Sunday 4th of July
trying to find fireworks that *you* never found.

And an abandoned Mexican restaurant.
The one with the crack in the window and the
cinnamon chips.

In the shade of the trees

I hate the way the sun hangs this time of year.
The way it comes through the trees in lines as I'm
driving.
As I blink through these dried up tears I'm still crying.
Under your illusion, everything illuminated,
Whole time, I'm in the shade.
I remember once,
I loved it all too much.
But I can't forget the way I watched it fade.

Nothing has changed

I remember a place I found long ago.
I'd never seen it before,
And haven't seen it ever since.
But I just keep driving this same old road,
Just hoping to find it,
To get just one more glimpse.

The same trees line the road,
I drive through their shade.
Over new cracks in the pavement,
Maybe ones *your* tires made.
And I pass by the house
With its broken windows,
And I try to imagine how it looked years ago.

Maybe it saw us drive by a few times,
When I was still innocent and you were still kind.
I remember the grass; it was vibrant
And green.
Just the way I'd hoped it would be.

You slipped away, but nothing else changed,
Except the cracks in the road
And the grass turned to gray.

Green kitchen

The kitchen walls were dusty and somber,
So I started to paint them
                            your favorite color.
During the winter, when everything was gray,
All I wanted was to find a place far, far away.

But you came along, the beginning of spring,
And made everything brighter than in all of my
dreams.
You put me back together, just to tear me apart
And pretended to love me, just playing a part.

The kitchen walls were halfway painted,
And you'd made up your mind while I held on and
waited.
The snow melts away slowly before the warm front
comes through,
And the grass beneath it dies, the damage hard to
undo.

That night on a drive, you said you couldn't fall in
love,
But then you played Presley,
And beat the wheel like the drums.
The sun comes out for a while but then begins to fade,
And the paint on the wall soon fades to gray.

I stare at the memories in my mind till I believe them
And regret the paint I wasted on this dark, empty
kitchen.
One day I dream you'll come take me out of this place
So I painted *our* kitchen green, just in case.

Things you won't say to me out loud

I miss you sometimes when I drive past your road.
I thought I could love you, but you'll never know.
Every now and then, I remember how you kiss
But I'd never understand you if it's me that you miss.

I know you can't forget me, the way you can't forget a scar.
And I'll reach for you when you walk away, so you never make it very far.
And sometimes I need you, so then I push you away.
Cause I don't know what love is, it's just a cliche.

I remember how you loved me when I play the radio
But you're better off without me, so just let me go.
And if I ever told you, you'd probably try to change my mind.
So I don't regret a single thing I said;
I've got too much pride.

If I still remember you when I go to *settle* down,
I'll pretend I always loved you, see if you're still around.
And I'll pull you in and make you laugh just how things were before
Until one day I get restless,
I won't love you anymore.

Plucking petals

I wasted all my falling stars just wishing for you.
And plucked all the petals from my daisies,
For an answer I already knew.
I've given you my heart and soul and everything I can
find,
So break my heart *again* so I don't waste this
Dandelion.

Rip me to shreds

I've torn myself apart trying to find the piece that you
didn't like
So I could throw it away and be every bit what you
wanted.
I'd rather you rip me to shreds than silently walk
away.
Anger is closer to love than apathy so I'd rather have
that,
Than none of you at all.

July

That night in July, you held me in your arms in the
driver's seat.
I knew it was over,
But I just kept pretending to be naive.
You played my favorite song through the speakers,
And I saw the regret through your eyes.
I'm afraid I'll always love you
And I'll always hate July.

I don't know how to leave you in the back of my
mind,
Cause I've never heard anything as beautiful as your
sweet   *little lies.*
I don't know how to find you cause my world's gotten
so dark,
But you're the thing I long for
When I wish on the stars.

I remember your eyes in the street lights those nights
in your car,
And the way that you felt just like home.
Sometimes I get stuck just reliving the feeling
Mourning someone that I never knew,
But I   *don't stop believing.*

I can't seem to separate you from your perfect
disguise
I'm afraid I'll always believe you,
And I'll always hate July.

Unrequited memories

I'm dancing in this kitchen with memories we never
made
Holding you, holding me,
As we sway.
I push and you pull, across the dusty hardwood floor.
Loving who you never were,
I just can't do this anymore.
I adore you,
Even more than I could love a song.
And I'd do anything for you,
Even though I know it's wrong.
Just for you to hold me in this room,
And dance me through this life
                    That's suffocating
                    without you.

My socks slide across the floor as you twirl me round
And then,
You kiss me softly like you did
So long ago, back when
You imagined I was the girl who could save you
From yourself.
But you read the book too fast,
So you put it on your shelf.
No words could save you from your misery,
Save you from the pain,
Or from the hidden hatred you have,
For everything.
In the beginning I guess you thought I'd be enough,
To distract you from the things you call mundane.
And from living every day over and over.
But I started to breathe,
As you started to smother.

We thought I'd be the one you'd want to change for,
But I turned out to be
just.
another.
bore.
But it was too late because I already adored you.
When you held me in my mind, just for a little while,
And danced me through this life
      That's suffocating
      Without you.

Your hand holds the back of my neck
And it feels like part of you might love me.
The lies we tell to keep from being lonely.
And I know now I loved you too soon
Cause I'd known you forever,
Somewhere inside my dreams.
But you'll never love me cause I just remind you of all
the things
That you want so desperately,
But you think you don't deserve.
You spin me in slow motion,
And everything's a blur.
I'm living in my fantasy,
And you're living in your nightmare
Cause I'm not the perfect girl you made,
I'll never be her.
Your image fades away
And I'm dancing in this empty kitchen
Falling on the floor.
The yellow lights turn gray, the record skips, and you
don't love me anymore.

But you never existed.
And neither did your love,

And neither does this kitchen.
I've been here dancing all alone forever.
Because even when you were here, you were so far
away.
But I adored you.
And you adored the games we played.
Burn down this house, and burn down this kitchen,
And let me suffocate.
In this smoke, in this life, I'm just a fool
                    That's suffocating
                    Without you.

I can't breathe,
I can't love, and I can't see.
The smoke surrounds me
Where you used to be.
It drowns you out,
And it's drowning me.
And my dreams become nightmares of
                    unrequited memories.

From the sea birds

Remember, I was young
And I ran along the beach from the sea birds.
Remember, I was young
I fell in love in the summer.
Remember, I was young
And I thought it would last forever
Remember, we were young
In your car, my hands in your hair.
When you were who I'd dreamed of
And love was more than fair.

Pile of Leaves

I think I could understand you more if you were
insane.
At least you'd have a better excuse to treat me this
way.
And I think I'd forgive myself a little better if there
was something more wrong with me,
Cause maybe it would explain my addiction to your
cruelty.

I need to hate you to let you go, but the person who
loved you won't let me.
I thought if I gave you everything that you wouldn't
remember how to forget me.
Sometimes I miss the feeling of running as fast as I
can, just to jump in a pile of leaves.
I miss not knowing what could lie there,
The endless hope of being naive.

Take a little more

I wish you didn't know a thing about me,
But then I wish you knew everything just to make you
understand
How my thoughts, they flutter, and the awful places
they choose to land.
And know the parts of every song that take me right
back to you.
And feel just how my stomach drops when something
dares remind me of the things you used to do.
I hate how you perceive me.
Come back and hold me for a second,
Just to leave me.

The way you push me out
Just to pull me right back in
Like an addiction I can't shake,
A bet I'll never win .
I guess I can't tell the difference
Between forgetting and forgiveness.
All you've given me is ingenuine love,
Then resistance.
All I've wanted to give you is everything.
So I've given you every thing.

I wish I could abhor you,
But I still just adore you.
Afraid I always will.
I think I understand your cruelty,
But I'm too naive to care.
I crave the pain you cause me,
At least it means you're there.
Every time you're back, you whittle away a little more
All I've given you is everything

Come take
a little more.

Unwanted weeds

Not enough words, too many things to say
I try to make them sound cold so you don't look away
I yearn for you
Like the moon yearns for darkness.
Like the weeds need the rain,
But no one wants them.

Between you and Heaven

I hate that I couldn't save you,
But you don't even believe that God can.
I know He already has.
And I wish I could make you believe it.
I wish I wasn't just another sin.
That you didn't regret me,
And repent for me the way you repent for your
wrongs,
Like I stand between you and Heaven.
The way *you* stand between me and what I once
thought was
mine.

I don't want to forget

I tried to find you in myself since you're not around
anymore.
But I ruined it because I'm just not the same.
And I think I love you still,
But I barely even know anything.
And you once said you're sorry but,
You don't even know my favorite color,
But I'm afraid I'll never be able to forget that yours is
Green.

And that night that I kissed you to "Hotel California,"
I loved you right then, I would've sworn it.
And your distant eyes were all I ever wanted.
I bet those memories are
Just something you lost.
I know you'd never look for them,
But I'd do anything to never…
Forget
        the cost.

I'm homesick

I dreamed about you last night,
You were holding me at arms length.
Just for a moment, you pulled me in to kiss me,
I opened my eyes, and you were gone.
Woke up for a moment and tried to go back to sleep,
To go back home.

Someone's been here before

I fell in love in the spring and more in the summer
Someone's said that before.
I felt my heart shatter
But someone's felt that before
I kissed you, and it felt like heaven
But someone must have done that before.
I'm stuck in my memories
In love with the ways you do everything
I've never loved this way before.

You put your arm around me, my head on your chest
But so many lovers have done that before.
I fell asleep while you held me, like you wanted to be
there.
No one's done that for *me* before.
You laughed and I watched you
The way I never saw anyone before.
You made me nervous, too nervous to speak
Everyone's been there, but not me, before.
We play the radio, I'm on your lap in the car
I've never seen anyone listen the way you do before.

You hold me so tenderly, then throw me away
I love you too much to hate all the games that you
play.
I've never forgiven the way I forgive you before
I love you in a way I can't explain, but even more.
I don't have the words to get out the things I have to
say.
I miss the summer as a little girl, just going outside to
play,
Nothing more.

I miss not knowing that you even exist, and the way
the world looked
Before.

I'm just a liar

You asked me if I knew "Doolin' Dalton" by the
Eagles,
And I said yes.
You asked me so I'd hear you every time it played,
So I'd never forget.
So now I think of you every time I hear my favorite
songs,
As if I didn't remember you enough already,
Long after you've been gone.

Once, you told me you didn't even know my favorite
color,
But you thought it might be blue.
I laughed as I lied and said I didn't know yours either,
But everything that's green still reminds me of you.

Sometimes I see you and we both look away,
Almost as though it were all just a mistake.
I wonder if you still have to sleep with a fan
And if I could've done better to make you understand.

And if you still hang all those trees on your visor
I don't care, it doesn't matter,
Or I'm just a liar.

Through your eyes

Whenever I look at myself through your eyes,
I hate every little thing that isn't wrong.
But when I look at you through my own,
I love everything that is.

Like growing up

This feeling isolates me,
No one understands how I love the way you hate me.
They say it wasn't all that serious, not to anyone but
me
But it feels like you took a piece of my soul,
The part I need to breathe.
The girl that I once was, grew up way too fast,
And the disguise you wore on April nights was way
too thin to last.
I yearn for you in the way that I miss my innocence.
I reach for you, grasping, for someone who does not
exist.

You reminded me of a place I found when I was
young
I think that's why losing you seemed to feel just like
growing up.
The way they make it sound easy to give you up and
let you go
Makes me wonder if they've ever been in love enough
to know.
And I wonder why I couldn't heal your self-inflicted
misery,
And I hate myself for it almost as much as you resent
me.

Vendetta

I wish the sound of the wind blowing
Past my window, on the road, didn't remind me of you
And racing you home on the backroads,
Just your taillights and the moon.

I wish I could get the sound of your laugh out of my
head,
And forget the creases in my sheets the night you held
me in my bed.
And stop feeling your smile on my lips.
And the touch of your hands on my hips.

Somehow all the little things are tainted by your
touch,
And I hear you in all the melodies,
How you haunt the things I love.

But I still listen to them and pretend you're by my
side.
Still feel your thumb rubbing back and forth on mine,
In the passenger seat where I still sit in the past.
And remember the way I looked at you,
And how you never looked at me like that.

But there's some place in time we'll always be
together,
And the love I had for you is something even you
can't sever.

Now I just listen to your favorite songs, like a
vendetta.
It's the only thing I've got left of when things were
better.

Nailing down wooden floors

When you left, I lost the memories
That we never *quite* made
Like holding your eyes down the aisle
As I walked on my wedding day.
Sometimes I remember a new home
And nailing down wooden floors,
But it must not be a memory of mine
If it's not a memory of yours.

On your birthday every year, I bake you a coconut pie,
And you drive me around to find fireworks
The night before every 4th of July.
I remind you of that summer all those years ago.
How I hold it in my fists,
I forgot to let it go.

And I can almost feel the softest wrinkles lying on
your skin.
Tonight I made the coffee but tomorrow's your turn
again.
All these nights I've learned to sleep to the drone of a
square, white fan
And your breath beside my ear under the comfort of
your hands.
And once I start remembering these things that'll
never be,
I forget that you're long gone,
And you were never in love
With me.

The dirt that falls

You love the way my hair sits,
When I do it just for you.
And I adore the dirt that falls from the soles of your
shoes.
You love the clothes I wear, when they land on the
floor,
And I find comfort in places, if you've been there
before.
I search for pieces of you in the people that you've
known,
Because I can't even find them in *you* now, since they
were never there at all.
But just for a moment in time, the world will stop in
its tracks.
You'll wear your gentle disguise and just for a
moment, you'll be back.
My mind finally understands, but my heart hasn't
been keeping score.
How many times do you have to break me until I can't
be put back together anymore?

Late October's depths

Late October, the air turns cold,
And only for a moment,
Your tenderness returns.
And you expect to see me falling right back in
Because you thought I'd never learn.
The words I'd yearned for all this time
Don't heal the way I thought they would,
Because to you,
They're just a way to right your wrongs
And convince yourself you're really good.
But your gentleness hurts me more than your cruelty
Because I know what lies in its depths,
And you know I hold a softness for you
That you yearn to take from till there's
Nothing left.

Nostalgia

You cured my nostalgia for the places I've never been,
And took me someplace I'd longed for,
But I don't know if I can ever go there again
Rubbed my thumb softly in your hand
And played your radio just loud enough
Watched as I fell so hard while you stood upright,
I unraveled, coming undone.
Feeling like a drive-in movie,
Watching my illusions playing out in real life
Holding me so gently I couldn't feel you
Cutting my soul just like a knife.

Like a songbird

My words I write
They fly away.
They have no place to land.
Like a songbird they flutter,
Hoping to mean something
The words I speak never can.

Bluffing

I bought a green sweater
And I did the *things you never could.*
And after all, I did it for you,
But it's no use.
I'm still no good.
And I hear "Oh Sherrie" in the grocery store
And remember your hands on a hinged glass door.
And a car ahead of me turned left down your road,
So I thought maybe it was you.
But the curve swallowed up my vision,
So I guess I never really knew.
I guess the love has turned into something like
nothing.
Oh I don't miss you at all anymore,
And I hope you can't tell that I'm bluffing.

Only in the film

I wish I could step into a polaroid
And hand myself to you
A version posed and entirely devoid
A person you never knew

The only way we will ever be
Is inside a picture frame
In a world where I'm up to your fantasy
A perfect contender in your games.

2:21

"I can't fight this feeling,"
And it's 2:21, our favorite part.
This yearning I'm concealing,
Slowly prying me apart.
The nostalgia pursues
And tells me that I can,
With anyone but you.

A battle you've already won

I've heard that misery loves company
And I found this morbid kind of peace
Knowing you left everyone else who loved you,
Ones much easier to love than me.

I saw her wearing a ponytail, beautiful like lace.
Long before I knew her, I could see it in her face
Gentleness and warmth and love for things unknown
And when that love looked toward you, she turned
and you were gone.

Her hair was golden like cattails and curled just like
the waves
And she was just the kind of girl your heart begins to
crave
And you put her on a pedestal, higher than the moon.
Until she fell all the way to the ground when she
began to fall for you.

And then your eyes turned toward me.
And they knew how to look, like your lips knew how
to speak
You knew the end before I even knew the beginning
You always jump off the carousel as soon as it begins
spinning.

The lights are blurring, I'm waiting on you to come
back on
But you'll never come back to a battle you've already
won.

Looking for you

I thought I might be able to love him
But I *knew* I loved you.
And he pulled me in close, and I resented his lips
against mine.
And I realized I was searching for your soul
In someone else's eyes.

I don't know you anymore

I look in your cold blue eyes and I can't find you
there.
Your gaze used to feel so soft, like the touch of your
hands in my hair.
And I try to say I don't love you anymore, but it gets
stuck in my throat
I regret that I've let myself be ruined, but not the
words that I once wrote.
You regret the sins that you've since pawned on me,
Regret me just like a
who're
you? I don't recognize you at all anymore.

Rainbow

When I was a child, my mother sang me to sleep to
"You are my Sunshine."
And in the mornings, the air hung peacefully with the
yellow shining through the blinds.
And my nana, she would call and invite us down the
path to eat some lunch.
And then at night, we'd watch the sunset, walking
down the road at dusk.
And sometimes when it rained, and the sun was
getting low,
My mom would point and say, "Hey look, there's a
rainbow."

And my father, he took us fishing in the evenings dim
and humid,
The water made its ripples against the setting sun with
her lumens.
And my papa held me in his warm coat on the way
back to the shore,
But then one day a nightmare came, and the cold air
made my lungs sore.
The nightmare turned the air to gray, and the sun
couldn't find the ground.
Until that one day when you made me laugh, for just a
moment, the sun peeked through the clouds.
And in your gaze, I almost forgot all the harsh things
I'd come to know.
And all the gray turned to pastel, and all I could see
was the light from the rainbow.

It seemed I'd grown up in just one night, when the air
was heavy with dew.

And suddenly I realized all these terrible things that as a child, I never knew.
Like how happy memories are the ones that leave you with the dullest ache,
Because you can't go back and visit them even if you go to the very same place.
But then you would *play me* the radio and sing the high notes in your white car,
And that peaceful haze of the air came back when I held the phone and you played the Eagles on your guitar.
The sun burned so brightly, like when it shines on freshly fallen snow.
Everything seemed to be alright, underneath the colors of the rainbow.

But then one day the leaves turned inside out as the rain started falling,
And the stars seemed to fall right out of the sky the night that you stopped calling.
So I wrote a letter on both sides of notebook paper, with a ballpoint pen,
And told you I loved all the little things about you, and the way that we had been,
But those words must not have mattered, because you still had to go.
The clouds covered up all that was left of the sun,
Because you brought back the rain, bow.

www.ingramcontent.com/pod-product-compliance
Lightning Source LLC
Chambersburg PA
CBHW030527130626
46549CB00007B/3137